# Psychology of Labyrinth:
## An Unofficial Exploration

Dr. Megan A. Arroll

ISBN-10: 1534657894
ISBN-13: 978-1534657892

## DEDICATION

This one's for Chloe—so grown-up but not quite grown.
Love you girl.

# CONTENTS

# ACKNOWLEDGMENTS

Thank you to my Ma who let us watch this, and many other movies over again…and again…and again. It must have driven you crazy. But more than that thank you for never squishing my imagination and giving us the freedom to explore—I still believe amazing things happen and true adventures are possible and this is because of you. Thanks also to my little Big sister who I'm sure wished me away numerous times as children but puts up with my antics pretty well now.

# PREFACE

Jim Henson's *Labyrinth* is a movie of my childhood. Filmed and released after Henson's *The Dark Crystal*, *Labyrinth* was produced by George Lucas of *Star Wars* fame and heavily influenced by the design and artistry of Brian Froud. The movie was a financial flop at the time, even with the pulling power of its rock star central baddie, David Bowie. This "failure" for Henson reportedly left him demoralized—it is clear from the intricacy of the movie that Henson, Froud, and the team put their heart and soul into it. Sadly, this was Henson's last feature film before his untimely death in 1990 and it breaks my heart that he would have never known how it has become a cult classic. For me, a scrawny, white-blonde-haired kid running around the desert in Arizona, *Labyrinth* encapsulated my fears, dreams, and desires. I truly believe Henson was a creative genius and this movie is a beloved classic in my eyes.

## Disclaimer

This book is an unofficial text and contains my personal views only. Apart from the characters in the film *Labyrinth*, any resemblance to actual persons, living or dead, or actual events is purely coincidental.

Although the author and publisher have made every effort to ensure that the information in this book was correct at press time, the author and publisher do not assume and hereby disclaim any liability to any party for any loss, damage, or disruption caused by errors or omissions, whether such errors or omissions result from negligence, accident, or any other cause.

# 1 WHO IS SARAH?

Early on in the movie it's clear that Sarah is a teenager and undoubtedly younger psychologically than some modern adolescents—bearing in mind this movie was released in 1986, arguably a slightly more innocent era that wasn't awash with smartphones, Snapchat, and sexting. Sarah appears from the very start to be somewhat of a fantasist who feels compelled to enter worlds other than those of her ordinary suburban surroundings. In the first scene, Sarah is alone except for her dog Merlin—she's not with other girls her age and is not doing the sorts of things teenage girls of this age might be expected to do, such as shopping and gossiping about boys. Therefore, we might think of Sarah as a bit of a loner and perhaps we can find clues as to why she may prefer a make-believe environment to the real world.

## Maternal separation

Once we enter Sarah's room, the frame focuses on various clippings related to her mother. It is most likely that Sarah's closest caregiver has passed away by the manner in which the newspaper clippings and photos are arranged; however, this is a guess and Sarah's mother could indeed be on tour with her production company. Regardless of why the mother is no longer present in Sarah's life, absence of this key role model is a fundamental driver for Sarah's behavior and beliefs about herself. Although it's never discussed explicitly, it's clear from the paraphernalia in Sarah's bedroom that her birth mother is an actress and has starred in numerous fairytale-like roles on the stage. Is this why Sarah identifies with fairy stories and characters so much? Sarah clearly loves and misses her mother deeply, and this love will be tangled with a sense of abandonment. This feeling of desertion, or rather dealing with the grief and abandonment issues that Sarah has, is a central tenet of the movie.

## Sarah's ambivalent attachment

There are different types of "attachment styles" that we develop from early childhood and which go on to mold our future adult relationships. As young children we learn about human relationships and concepts such as trust, security, and the confidence to explore the world from our primary caregiver – most often our mothers but fathers, grandparents, and other adults can fill this role too. There are four main categories of attachment style (secure, avoidant, ambivalent, and disorganized) and these different kinds of attachment styles will produce differing outcomes. In terms of Sarah, she's clearly very fond of her mother (we are assuming her mother was her primary caregiver although it is noted that she lives with her father now) and emulates her. We see this from the theatrical costumes and also the fact that Sarah is learning monologues. From these clues we can assume that Sarah's mother was absent from home during her childhood which could have resulted in an "ambivalent attachment style." This type of attachment style formed in childhood can produce insecurities and self-doubt in adulthood and anger and possessiveness in adolescence.

Sarah as a "moody teenager"

If we now understand Sarah in terms of her ambivalent attachment style, her behavior starts to make sense. She's very rude towards her father and stepmother when she comes in from the rain and storms upstairs. This, of course, may simply be a reflection, but we do know that adolescent girls with an ambivalent attachment style can experienced mood instability. In other words, girls who have developed this attachment style are more likely to be "moody," throw tantrums and shout and slam doors than girls with a secure or avoidant type of attachment. Sarah's rage over her much loved teddy bear Lancelot being with her baby brother and this type of possessiveness over her belongings can also be appreciated as the consequence of the attachment style and not because she's a spoilt girl.

Sarah's father

We don't know why Sarah's parents are no longer together; he may be a widower or the couple may have divorced. They could have even fallen out of love or Sarah's stepmother could have come onto the scene and triggered a breakdown in the family unit—we just don't know for certain. But we do know that Sarah's father appears to be a caring man and a family man as he's provided a comfortable home for his brood. Also, he tries to talk to Sarah when she's upset, rather than merely letting her stew in her fury. Sarah's reaction to her father again demonstrates her ambivalent attachment style—she wants him to come and comfort her but slams the door in his face. Sarah perhaps needs a quest in order to figure out what is important in her life…

Sarah's stepmother

When Sarah storms up the stairs after coming in from her roleplay to babysit, her stepmother is exasperated with being treated like the evil nemesis in Sarah's story. Sarah's father must have been married to her stepmother for some time since they have a child (Toby), so there would have been opportunity for the two females to bond. The lack of a positive relationship, even though the stepmother is clearly trying to identify with Sarah (she mentions dating but this isn't taken well, as can be imagined), is yet another sign of the complexity, mistrust and uncertainty Sarah feels in her life and everyday world.

Toby

Now we turn to Toby. Sarah's baby brother is both the object of her resentment and the key to overcoming her demons. Toby represents not only the loss of her mother but also Sarah's future; if she doesn't deal with her difficult feelings and ambivalent attachment style, she will remain a little girl and not be able to develop into an adult woman. So in this interpretation of Sarah and her reality we can perceive Toby as the agent for change and development that Sarah so desperately needs. The name Toby stems from Tobias which is taken from Tobiyah and means "God is good." Therefore, Toby is quite possibly Sarah's overseer and protector, in a figurative sense, even though it is Sarah that must save Toby from the Goblin King.

Lancelot

In Arthurian legend, Sir Lancelot was one of the Knights of the Round Table. Lancelot was King Arthur's trusted companion until he embarked on an adulterous affair with Queen Guinevere, which gave rise to the fabled civil war that eventually consumed Arthur's kingdom. In the movie, Lancelot can be seen as the catalyst to Toby's abduction by Jareth, following Sarah's request to take him away. Therefore, Lancelot can be understood as the trigger to the entire encounter between Sarah and Jareth, as the toy was secretly nestling with Toby. But rather than an adult partner as in the Arthurian legend, here Lancelot can be viewed as the symbol of Sarah's childhood which she feels her half-brother Toby is trying to steal away from her.

### Sarah's need for the Labyrinth

Now that we know a little of Sarah's underlying character, in particular her attachment style, we can view the need to recuse Toby from the Goblin King not as a literal mission but as an important developmental vehicle for Sarah's life. When Sarah first meets Hoggle at the beginning of the Labyrinth and the small goblin asks her if she's going into the maze, Sarah replies that yes, she must—and indeed she, like the rest of us, has to grow up and enter the adult world, painful as that may be.

In the next chapter we explore what the creatures and also what Jareth signifies in Sarah's journey.

.

# 2 WHO IS JARETH?

The simply answer to this of course is "The Goblin King," but that tells us little of our antihero's character. On the surface, Jareth is selfish, self-serving, and utterly self-centered—an egotist who should attract none of our sympathy. But, of course, this is not accurate because we do care about this seemingly cruel central figure.

Jareth is the owl

At both the beginning and end of the movie Jareth is an owl. In Native American teachings the owl is a spirit messenger who brings dreams, so this may be a literal interpretation of Jareth as the owl since he offers Sarah the opportunity of obtaining her dreams—at the cost of Toby. However, owls also represent wisdom and intuition, they can also signify change, and, perhaps more notable in this context, life transition. In Greek mythology the owl is sacred to the goddess Athena who, in addition to being the godness of wisdom, also stands for courage, strength, skill, law and justice, and heroic endeavor. These are all themes throughout the film and we can see how Sarah, through her journey and transition, grows in strength and skill, and starts to understand the at times confusing laws (or lack there of) within the Labyrinth. For Athena, the owl is a companion who exposes concealed truths to the goddess so that she may see the complete picture and speak the whole, rather than a partial, truth. So, taken from this perspective, we might view Jareth as Sarah's guide on her journey through the Labyrinth who helps Sarah see aspects of herself that she has buried deep within and, as such, is a catalyst for much needed growth.

In other mythology-based belief systems such as that of Ancient Egypt, owls can also embody guardianship of souls passing from the living world to the underworld. Indeed the song that tops and tails the film and performed by David Bowie is called "Underground."[1] This interpretation brings us back to a consideration of Sarah's mother and we might view the owl and Jareth as a channel by which Sarah can overcome the loss of her mother by processing her grief. This can even be taken a step further as the owl could be understood as Sarah's mother herself, in a form trapped between this world and the next, waiting and overseeing Sarah until she has completed her quest.

Jareth as the reality checker
Jareth only arrives when he is summoned by Sarah. Although she doesn't use the correct phrase initially to call on the goblins after dealing with Toby's fussing, when she leaves the baby's room Sarah's deepest and darkest true feelings have heard the words the goblins have whispered: this allows our female protagonist to successfully request the child's removal. It is only at this point that Jareth arrives, disguised as an owl, and does exactly what Sarah has wished for. In other words Jareth is merely acting on Sarah's request. Haven't we all secretly desired something

---

[1] Bowie, D. (1989). Underground. On *From the original Soundtrack Labyrinth* [CD]. Hollywood, CA: EMI America Records.

that we'd be gravely ashamed of if it actually came to fruition? Wishing the demise of a friend's or colleague's relationship, slyly hoping that our siblings fail at something, or even worse—while we would be mortified if these things did indeed happen after daydreaming about them, it's perfectly normal and natural to have such thoughts. But if harm were indeed to befall the intended, it would be a different matter. Therefore, Jareth can be viewed as a form of "reality check"—Sarah, of course, didn't want her brother to disappear, even if that was her heart's deepest desire at the moment she turned off his bedroom light.

## Jareth as the dream maker

But Jareth can also be perceived as the conduit to Sarah's dreams. These have been captured in a crystal and we can only imagine what they might be. Perhaps to see her mother again. Perhaps to be a child again. Don't we all crave the warmth and security of a mother's care, such as we had when children, at times? On a darker side perhaps Sarah wishes to become the Goblin Queen—there are certainly hints of a romance and longing between the two main characters. Jareth points out that the spherical crystal is not a present for an average girl who looks after a crying baby, implying that Sarah is somehow better than this—special even in his eyes. Indeed if Sarah hands over Toby, she may leave her life of drudgery. Hence the intimation is that by making her dreams come true Sarah could eclipse her ordinary life, and who hasn't fantasized about that?

## Who, not what

But these analyses are really asking 'What is Jareth to Sarah', not an evaluation of the man himself. So next we will try to unravel the mysterious character played by the late David Bowie.

<u>Was Jareth suffering from a personality disorder?</u>
We know nothing of Jareth's background—why is he the only human in his kingdom? Why does he have the need to collect children and turn them into goblins? Why can't they stay as children? How does he know what Sarah's dreams are?

In a real-world analysis Jareth might be categorized as someone with a narcissistic personality disorder. This is a serious psychiatric condition so by no means does discussing this type of issue in relation to a fictional character negate the gravity of such illnesses; this is simply for descriptive purposes.

According to the *Diagnostic and Statistical Manual of Mental Disorders*, 5th ed. (DSM-5),[2] which is the American Psychiatric Association's classification system of mental disorders, one of the main aspects of narcissistic personality disorder is the need for approval from others and there is often little awareness of internal motivations. At the end of the movie, Jareth implores: "I ask for so little. Just fear me. Love me. Do as I ask, and I shall be your slave,"[3] clearly demonstrating what psychologists would call an "impairment in self-direction": Jareth is unable to set goals without the attention of others and also has an unrealistic sense of entitlement. This is an abnormal type of "self functioning" which also includes an impairment with regard to identity. At many points in the movie Jareth uses excessive reference to his goblins for self-definition. This is particularly apparent in the Goblin King's interactions with Hoggle, whom he knows Sarah is fond of: "You don't think a young girl could ever like a repulsive little scab like you?"[3] is a striking example of an exaggerated self-appraisal made

---

[2] American Psychiatric Association (2013). *Diagnostic and Statistical Manual of Mental Disorders* (5th ed.). Arlington, VA: American Psychiatric Publishing.
[3] Labyrinth (1986). Directed by Jim Henson [Film]. USA: TriStar Pictures.

by contrasting to a reference point, here the lowly (although not-so-lowly in the end) Hoggle.

Then there are "impairments of interpersonal functioning" within the DSM-5 criteria for narcissistic personality disorder that we can explore in relation to Jareth. First let's consider the trait of empathy—the psychiatric definition is the same as the everyday meaning, i.e. knowing how others feel and being able to instinctively understand the needs of others. For someone with this type of personality disorder, empathy is a problem; it's either nonexistent or a person with this diagnosis can be incredibly attuned to how people around them react but only when these reactions are relevant to that person. There can also be an overblown sense of the effects a person with narcissistic personality disorder believes they have on others. Does this sound like Jareth at all???

There is also the issue of intimacy. The DSM-5 states that the relationships someone with this condition has are predominately superficial, existing to serve as a boost to self-esteem rather than a healthy reciprocal connection. Often a narcissistic personality disorder is typified by a lack of genuine interest in other people and an overarching concern with personal gain. Jareth is not prepared to forsake Toby and indeed wants Sarah to both fear and love him. This is far from an equitable relationship and yet again demonstrates that Jareth could be considered to have a narcissistic personality disorder.

Finally, there is grandiosity and attention seeking, both of which Jareth's entire world has been constructed to feed.

# 3 WHO IS HOGGLE?

Hoggle ultimately becomes Sarah's friend, but within the story he is also her guide. Hoggle is aware of the laws of the land as can be seen when he's spraying the fairies—Sarah at first thinks this is cruel until one bites her. Hoggle, who knows this world and is not at all surprised by the fairies' aggression, responds to Sarah's sarcasms, demonstrating his superiority in this situation. So we know from the outset that this companion is streetwise, at least in the ways of the Labyrinth. Hoggle even seems to know who Sarah is before she introduces herself and does not appear at all alarmed to see this new person in the Labyrinth. Therefore, in this sense we can perhaps view Hoggle as an aspect of Sarah, even part of her psyche.

Hoggle as the "Id"
In Freudian psychoanalytic theory the psyche, which is basically our personality, is comprised of three components: the id, ego, and superego. These facets interact and work together to contribute and result in a person's outwardly behavior, so we can infer aspects of the human psyche by overt actions. The id is the most basic and immature part of

the psyche (Freud's theory was mainly about human development) and works mainly on the basis of instincts rather than via rational thought processes. The id is also selfish and we can see this in Hoggle's behavior when he desires Sarah's jewelry and becomes quite moody when she gives a ring to the Wiseman. If we think about Hoggle (and other characters to follow) as reflecting aspects of Sarah's personality, Hoggle at the beginning of the Labyrinth is certainly the most irrational and reactive creature[4] and almost until the final battle within the Goblin City appears jealous of Sarah's friendship with the other Labyrinth characters.

Hoggle as Jareth's henchman

Throughout the movie Jareth bullies and intimidates Hoggle. But how far will Hoggle go to avoid the wrath of Jareth? There is a classic study in the field of social psychology that was conducted by Stanley Milgram in the 1960s at Yale University in New Haven, Connecticut. This experiment was devised by Milgram because he wanted to understand the atrocities of World War II and how so many men could have followed Hitler's orders and carried out such terrible acts. In the early 1960s there was a trial of Adolf Eichmann, the German Nazi who was one of the major organizers of the Holocaust, so it was a very hot topic at the time. The aim of the study was to see if an ordinary man would obey an authority figure even if it meant causing physical pain to another person. This experiment has been replicated many hundreds of times with numerous variations, but the main results stay the same— people in general will follow orders from someone in charge, even if this means harming another individual. Thus, even though Hoggle maintains that he wouldn't ever

---

[4] In the strictest reading of the Id and Freudian theory, this factor does not change and is unconscious, so this is an interpretation.

hurt Sarah when Jareth gives him the Poisoned Peach, he does in fact deliver the dangerous fruit to Sarah in the forest.

Hoggle as the flawed friend

Hoggle openly admits that he's cowardly and afraid of Jareth, and this honesty leads us to empathize with the goblin. We are all frightened at times and it can be very difficult to show courage. We see Hoggle open up to Sarah when he says rather mournfully that he's never had a friend before he met her. But when scared Hoggle reverts back to his place of safety of only serving himself. Furthermore, Sarah finds Hoggle hard to trust after she finds out that Jareth instructed him to lead her back to the beginning of the Labyrinth. But there's no denying that most of Hoggle's unscrupulous deeds are those which Jareth has forced upon him through fear of the Bog of Eternal Stench and his more subtle manipulation via belittlement and denigration. In this respect, even Hoggle's most destructive actions are understandable, and he is far from an unsympathetic character.

Hoggle's battle with Humongous

Humongous is a mechanical creature that protects the Goblin City and lies just inside its gates. This machine is in fact controlled by a small goblin who works levers and pulleys in its head, which is a straightforward analogy for the human brain. Hoggle bravely pulls the head off the giant and throws out the goblin but can't quite control Humongous. This doesn't matter since Sarah forgives him for giving her the Poisoned Peach, Sir Didymous commends Hoggle for his courage, and Ludo says they're now firm friends. So here, at this late stage in the journey, Hoggle becomes more than a mere henchman:  he blossoms into a hero in his own right.

# 4 WHO IS SIR DIDYMUS?

Sir Didymus is most likely a fox terrier and the Labyrinth character is true to this breed—fox terriers are known to be fearless and won't back down if confronted. Indeed, they often challenge other animals and can be particularly stubborn. When the group reaches the gates of the Goblin City, Sir Didymous is rather too eager to get in and yells at the sleeping guards as well as banging their helmets, quite an unwise move on his part but completely in keeping with his breed.

Ambrosius

We first meet Sir Didymous and his trusted, although spineless, steed Ambrosius in the Bog of Eternal Stench. Interestingly, Ambrosius is the same type of dog as Merlin (a Bearded Collie) and it is no coincidence that "Ambrosius" is another name that the great wizard in the legend of King Arthur used. Merlin was also a wise magician who prophesized that whoever drew the sword from the stone was King Uther's (Arthur's father) true heir and would rule Britain in post-Roman times. As the legend goes Merlin later became Arthur's close confidant and advisor.

Furthermore, in Greek "dídymos" means twin or double, and in biological sciences this word refers to something that is in pairs or two parts. Therefore, not only can we surmise that Merlin and Ambrosius are one and the same, but also that Sir Didymus and Ambrosius are two sides of the same coin. Whereas Sir Didymus is unwaveringly courageous, Ambrosius is cowardly and runs from conflict, only engaging in the final battle in Goblin City when his master threatens not to feed him. But no one is completely brave or entirely weak; we all have aspects of strength paired with our individual limitations.

### Sir Didymus as a Knight of the Realm

At the gates of Goblin City Sir Didymus also asks Sarah for reassurance about his bravery and skill before he quietens down, but we know Sir Didymous to be very brave and bold from the scene in the Bog of Eternal Stench—this is in keeping with the qualities of great knights who are also faithful, loyal, and honorable. These are all virtues that the plucky fox terrier exhibits. Furthermore, after his battle with Ludo in the Bog, where Sir Didymus exclaims that he and the beast should fight as one from now on, there is no doubt that he would fight to the death to protect and serve his chums. These features and his attire, in addition to the use of the name Ambrosius, undoubtedly demonstrate that this character stems from Arthurian legend.

### Sir Didymus as the "Ego"

However, Sir Didymus may also be thought of as a trait of Sarah herself, because if we remember at the beginning of the movie we only see Sarah with Merlin, not with any human friends or companions. In the previous chapter on Hoggle, we started to explore the Freudian theory of personality. If we consider that the main companions that accompany Sarah through the Labyrinth are aspects of her psyche, then Sir Didymus would be the Ego. Here the term "ego" does not mean a sense of self-esteem or self-worth as it does in everyday language, but the ego is another element of the self according to Freud. The function of the Ego is to reconcile the instinctive, and at times unreasonable, desires of the Id and the real world. Therefore the Ego is rational and takes into account society's views, customs, and rules when making decisions. We know that Sir Didymus is a stickler for the rules when he tells Sarah that she isn't allowed to cross the bridge without his permission. Yet he is also logical and reasonable, because when Sarah simply asks for permission rather than trying to fight her way past, Sir Didymus actually grants consent. Also, Freud compared the Ego to a man on horseback,[5] which may be why Sir Didymus rides Ambrosius (he is the only main character to do so and considering that he's a dog, there really isn't a great need for assistance in walking/running).

## Anosmia

Sir Didymus has a condition called anosmia, which is the complete loss of the sense of smell. This is quite advantageous for him since he lives and works in the Bog of Eternal Stench, but for most people this is a distressing condition. Disturbance in this sense affects the ability to taste; therefore it can actually be dangerous if, for example, food was contaminated or had started to spoil. Other dangers could potentially be the inability to notice the smell of smoke or a gas leak, however Sir Didymus appears completely unaware that he lacks this sense. Hence, although Sir Didymus is courageous to a fault, he does not always notice peril.

---

[5] Freud, S. (1961). *The ego and the id*. In J. Strachey (ed. and trans.), *The Standard Edition of the Complete Psychological Works of Sigmund Freud* (Vol. 19, pp. 3–66). London: Hogarth Press. (Original work published 1923)

# 5 WHO IS LUDO?

Ludo is one of the less complex characters in the Labyrinth. However, like most aspects of the story, Ludo is not what he seems. Although he looks like a beast, he is in fact the most gentle and thoughtful of creatures, showing us that appearances can be deceiving. Ludo and Sarah are friends immediately as she overcomes any fear of him, knowing by this point in her journey that the Labyrinth throws up many surprises. This is a decision she certainly would not regret as Ludo is steadfast in his friendship. However, when questioned, he doesn't know the way to the castle beyond Goblin City, but he is on Sarah's side from the get-go and there is never the lack of trust between this pair as was found with Hoggle and his more complicated nature.

### Ludo the game

The name Ludo is also that of a classic board game. In this square game that is made up of four sections for each player, dice are rolled in order to race to the center finishing square. This is a relatively simple game of chance derived from the traditional Indian game Pachisi, first seen in this modified form in England in the 19th century. There is no real skill involved since the pieces move on the basis of the rolled dice. The simplicity of this game is mirrored in Ludo himself—he is not as outwardly fearless as Sir Didymous and his trepidation in the forest is plain to see. Indeed Sarah comments on this, wondering at how such a big creature could be scared, demonstrating to us again that Ludo's feelings are pure and unadulterated by the Labyrinth. Also, it perhaps is no coincidence that Sarah meets him just after Hoggle is given orders by Jareth to take Sarah back to the start of the Labyrinth. In the Ludo game, if a player lands on a square that is already occupied by another player, the player on that spot must return to his/her home base.

Ludo as The "Superego"

If Hoggle is the Id and Sir Didymus the Ego, then in the Freudian theory of the human psyche, Ludo is the Superego. The Superego is aware of the morals and values of its surrounding and abides by these. In Ludo, we see someone who knows the ways of the Labyrinth and behaves appropriately in given situations. In psychoanalytic theory the Superego is comprised of the conscious and ideal self and so we can think of Ludo as this aspect of Sarah. He is brave and engages in battle when he must but does not feel the need to hide his feelings—which some may construe as weakness, e.g. his fear. Ludo seems completely at ease with himself and doesn't need to please anyone, certainly not Jareth. The Superego also represents the ethical component of our personalities and, again, we can appreciate that Ludo acts fairly throughout the movie.

The Rocks

When we think of rocks, we think of stability and reliability, of unmoving commitment and dependability. The late and tragic Princess Diana, first wife of Charles, Prince of Wales, who is currently first in line to the throne of England and Wales, famously said that her butler Paul Burrell was her rock. When this private and very intimate detail of Diana's platonic relationship was made public, we all immediately knew what was meant—she purportedly could rely on Burrell like no other and trusted him unreservedly. He later sold his story and ended up disgraced as the very qualities that his employer valued in him most were exchanged for money. But the use of the word "rock" in terms of relationships is clear; Ludo states that rocks are friends and when his safety is most threatened he calls on the Rocks for help. The Rocks really do help Ludo and his friends in the trickiest situations, offering a path out of the Bog of Eternal Stench, assisting in the battle within the Goblin City gates, and functioning as ammunition when Sarah is trying to save Ludo from the goblins who have tied him up and are attacking him with Nipper Sticks.

# 6 WORDS OF WISDOM...OR NOT

There are many red herrings and much misdirection within the Labyrinth. A great deal of this is physical: for example, how Ludo looks like a grisly beast but is in fact a calm and gentle escort and the pretty fairies at the gates at the start of Sarah's journey are actually more akin to biting insects than grant-wishing nymphs. Residents of the Labyrinth also impede Sarah's progress: for example, the Brick Keepers are small people who live under the stone paving of the maze and change her markings, markings that she's made so that she can ensure she doesn't go around in circles getting nowhere. However, some creatures that seem to be trying to trick Sarah and push her off course on this journey are actually benefiting her in terms of personal development and maturity. Therefore, we can view these characters as representing features of some well-known psychological therapies.

## The Worm
The Worm who lives with his wife in the Labyrinth walls is a very jolly English fellow indeed. He is the first to say explicitly that not all of what is encountered in this maze is

what it first appears to be—and that nothing should be taken on face value. By helpfully showing Sarah that the Labyrinth walls, which appear to be only a long corridor, actually have openings, she can get on her way to Goblin City. In cognitive therapy this is called "reframing," showing people that it is possible to look at a situation in a different light. This shift into a more positive perspective can be an important tool to strengthen ourselves mentally when faced with the many challenges in life.

But the Worm's lesson doesn't end there. In Sarah's haste to find Toby, the Worm tells her to go in the exact opposite direction to the castle. The worried manner in which the Worm tells Sarah that she should never go the way she was headed doesn't give the impression that he's trying to trick her, more that he's concerned for her well-being. If we understand the Labyrinth as a journey of growth for Sarah, then had she gone straight to the castle initially, she would not have experienced all the obstacles and overcome them. This is very similar to a therapist's role: s/he would not simply direct clients to an endpoint but guide them through what can be difficult recollections and feelings in order to learn and heal.

## The Wiseman and the Hat

More characters in the movie give Sarah advice. The Wiseman and his Hat tell her "sometimes the way forward is also the way back."[6] In psychotherapy, people are encouraged to discuss and even relive past traumatic events in order to proceed in life. If we consider Sarah's mother to have passed away and the Labyrinth to be in part at least a process to overcome her grief, this seems sage advice. The Wiseman also infers that getting to where you want to be can take time and at points it may feel that no progress is

---

[6] Labyrinth (1986). Directed by Jim Henson [Film]. USA: TriStar Pictures.

being made. This is very much in keeping with the practice of psychological therapy. To deal with deeply ingrained feelings and painful experiences is difficult—but it is possible. In this respect, the Wiseman and the Hat offer hope of resolution, but at a price because Sarah pays for these words of wisdom with her ring. This transaction frustrates Hoggle immensely which is consistent with the conception of this goblin as the Id portion of human psyche since it wants things only for itself and cares not for societal norms which state that services should be fairly remunerated.

<u>The Junk Lady</u>
After Sarah breaks free from the masked ball, she lands in a junkyard. Here she bumps into the Junk Lady who asks Sarah where she's going. Because she took a bite out of the Poisoned Peach (see Chapter 8), she can't remember where she is but vaguely recollects that she was searching for something. The Junk Lady tells Sarah in a rather agitated voice: "You can't look where you're going if you don't know where you're going!"[6] which like the Wiseman is essentially good counsel. This type of goal setting is important in contemporary psychological therapies, particularly cognitive behavioral therapy (CBT). Without having end points by which to measure progress, it can be very hard to see how far we have come and therapy can become somewhat circular. By having small, attainable goals, motivation to change can be maintained and an end kept in sight. This structured approach is a key difference between this more modern therapeutic technique and traditional psychotherapy.

So if we think of the Junk Lady as a therapist, she presents Lancelot bear to Sarah (which we have said represents the childhood that Toby has tried to snatch away from her), this can be viewed as the Junk Lady challenging Sarah's beliefs. The Junk Lady then leads Sarah to a door which opens onto her bedroom at home and at this point Sarah thinks for a moment that the entire ordeal has been a dream. She could regress here and go back to her former self before the Labyrinth began. But when the Junk Lady shows Sarah her toys and treasures and says that these material possessions are all Sarah has ever cared about in the world, we can see just how much Sarah has matured as she rejects this assertion. Instead of reverting back to her childish self, Sarah throws off the playthings, knickknacks, and make-up the Junk Lady has piled upon her and screams that all these possession are trash, remembering that she must save her baby brother. We can now see that Sarah's worldview has developed and she now believes that the people in her life right now are more important than holding onto past.

Taken together, the three characters of the Worm, the Wiseman, and the Junk Lady can be perceived as elements of psychological therapy. The paths that such therapy takes us on may not seem clear at the start, but a skilled therapist will challenge and guide the patient in order to find solutions and a way forward.

# 7 PUZZLES WITHIN PUZZLES

The Labyrinth is awash with puzzles and riddles, all set to test Sarah's commitment to her quest to save Toby and also stretch her intellectually. Although we play games and puzzles in childhood, life can be thought of as a series of conundrums for which we need to make decisions to "solve." Sarah encounters numerous creatures who pose dilemmas for her and ask her to select her route through the Labyrinth, often trying to persuade her to return to her past.

## The Door Knockers (Right and Left)

When Sarah and Ludo come upon a pair of doors, she stares at them wondering which one to choose. She asks the two Door Knockers what awaits beyond their posts, but they don't know what's behind the doors. Interestingly, one of them can't hear because he has a knocker in his ears and the other cannot speak since his knocker is in his mouth. Taking this together with the knowledge that neither of the Knockers can see what they lead to, we can surmise that these pieces of door furniture represent the principle of "see no evil, hear no evil, speak no evil" which is normally exemplified by the Three Wise Monkeys. There are many interpretations of this proverb, but as we are considering the Labyrinth to be a journey of growth, let's take the most upbeat and constructive version—that by striving to say good things, seeing actions in a positive light, and ignoring the negative words of others, it is possible to live a good life and steer clear of bad influences (evil). People who set out to do harm to others often fall into their own traps by looking for the worst in situations, listening out for criticism and denigration, and speaking badly of others. By always attempting to be positive in what we say, see, and hear, these hazards can be avoided.

The Right Door Knocker also teaches Sarah a further lesson: "Knock, and the door will open."[7] Not all doors will be wide open for us in life: some we will need to knock on to gain entry, some we might have to break down, and others we may need to create for ourselves. Because Sarah doesn't know what's behind each door, she's not sure at first which to choose. This is yet another learning experience for Sarah as she progresses through the Labyrinth—you may not know exactly what the future holds, but that shouldn't stop you stepping through the door.

## The Four Guards

The strange looking dog-like creatures that make up the Four Guards are based on a puzzle of logic called "Knights and Knaves." Originally this conundrum was set on an island where all of the residents were either knights or knaves and wherein the knights can only tell the truth when asked a question, but the knaves are only able to lie. A knave is another word for a dishonest man and also another term for a jack in a deck of cards, so this makes sense (the

---

[7] Labyrinth (1986). Directed by Jim Henson [Film]. USA: TriStar Pictures.

Guards' armor also looks like playing cards). So when a visitor comes to the island, or in this instance when Sarah meets the Four Guards, she must deduce the answer to her based on the fact that the knight will answer truthfully and the knave will fib. The Guards shield two doors, one that leads to the castle where Toby is held prisoner by Jareth and the other to certain death, and Sarah must figure out which one to choose. The two Guards at the bottom don't know the answer and she can only ask one of the Guards at the top a question about which door leads to the castle. So after careful consideration, Sarah asks a question that should force the Guards to give the same answer and she is actually correct in her approach. However, when Sarah pushes open the door behind the blue Guards, she still falls down a hole towards the oubliette. What does this encounter tell us, if Sarah appears to get the answer wrong even though it was right? Before Sarah passes the Guards, she brags that she's getting smarter, so this can be construed as a lesson to show how pride comes before a fall. But actually Sarah doesn't fall to her death and eventually reaches the castle, just not as quickly as she would have envisioned after figuring out the logic puzzle (but this, of course, is the Labyrinth and nothing is as it seems).

Helping Hands

As Sarah plummets down this hole, she is caught by a myriad of Helping Hands. These creatures offer Sarah the opportunity to go back up the way she fell or to continue downward. She doesn't know then that by choosing to go the way she's already pointing, i.e. down, leads to the oubliette. After correctly solving the Knights' and Knaves' brainteaser yet still plunging in darkness, it would be understandable if Sarah felt disheartened and demoralized, but here she shows us her staunchness and spirit by simply accepting this turn of events and following the path ahead (or rather below). We are reminded here that even though

Sarah may have much to learn, she does possess an innate strength of character and is committed to finding Toby.

## False Alarms

Like many characters in the Labyrinth, False Alarms are not what they seem. These stone carvings tell Sarah she's going the wrong way and that she must turn back, otherwise she will continue to certain destruction. Hoggle confides in Sarah, letting her know that there are many types of false alarms in the Labyrinth, particularly if she's going the right way. Doubt is a common feeling when we are advancing through life and it can sometime stop us short of going down new avenues. The famous poem 'The Road Not Taken'[8] by the American poet Robert Frost contains the frequently used lines "I took the one less traveled by, And that has made all the difference."[8] This is often interpreted as a call to free thinkers, travelers, and wanderers to explore the world. However, the poem has also been construed as a message which states it is futile to rake over the past and constantly replay earlier choices over and over in our minds: i.e. regrets are useless and we should live in the here and now, moving forward. It is human nature to analyze the past, but if too much time is spent on this activity it is known as "rumination." Ruminative thinking is common in disorders such as depression and anxiety and therefore it is important to break these negative thought patterns and not fear decisions. We can overthink just about anything in life, but this process rarely leads us anywhere. Therefore, the False Alarms, who admit that they are merely doing their jobs and saying scripted speeches from Jareth, teach us to walk on and not fear the future.

There are really no completely "right" or "wrong" choices in life. We make the best decisions with the

---

[8] Frost, R., & Untermeyer, L. (2002). *Robert Frost's Poems*. New York, NY: St. Martin's Paperbacks.

information we have at the time and most experiences can offer us some sort of knowledge— only if we choose to view it this way.

# 8 SEX, DRUGS, AND ROCK & ROLL

Sarah is a teenager, and this is a time of great transition and development, both emotionally and physically. These can be some of the toughest years for young people, when they try and find out where they fit in and who they are, as well as juggling the practicalities of school and home life. In addition to all this, Sarah is dealing with the grief from the loss of her mother and complex feelings stemming from her father's new marriage and now merged family. Many adolescents with this much on their plate might drift astray, and there are specific signs in the Labyrinth that indicate the dangers that Sarah might face in the real world and also in her blossoming sexuality.

## The Fireys

After Ludo disappears in the forest, Sarah is alone again when she crosses the path of the Fireys. The Fireys are a group of five creatures that really seem to like to party. Their red coats can be perceived as a signal of danger and Sarah is wary of them from the start. They sing and dance to the song "Chilly Down"[9] and during this track they remove various parts of their bodies. Hallucinations, delusions, and feeling separate from one's own body are phenomena associated with drug-taking. Indeed since the phrase "off your head" is used to imply when someone is high on drugs, we may understand this gang as a group with a substance misuse problem. Further evidence of this is when one of the Fireys rolls his "dice" (these are actually his eyes in a rather gruesome scene), which come up as "red eyes"—red, watery eyes with very large or very small pupils are a common sign of drug abuse. The gang try to entice Sarah to also take her head off by showing her how fun it is, but, of course, she cannot do this. Therefore, this entire interaction between the Fireys and Sarah can be viewed as our heroine rejecting the offer of illegal drugs even though the excitable creatures say that this exchange is free of charge. Some drug pushers use this technique to get people hooked on substances, i.e. let "customers" try the drug for free so that they become addicted. There are further lyrics in the song that imply drug-taking and overall this encounter can easily be translated to "if you're feeling stressed 'chill out' by taking substances that have relaxing or sedative qualities." The important aspects of this whole meeting between the Fireys and Sarah are the complete rejection of the offer to "chilly down" and also how Hoggle helps Sarah escape from these rather insistent creatures. Good friends can offer what is known as "social support" to people when they are at their lowest and most stressed, meaning that the temptation to use substances can be curbed. In fact, this type of support is important in just about all aspects of life and helps us to stay well and grounded.

---

[9] Bowie, D. (1989). Chilly Down. On *From the original Soundtrack Labyrinth* [CD]. Hollywood, CA: EMI America Records.

## The Poisoned Peach

Poisoned fruit is a familiar tool in fairy tales. In Snow White, the Evil Queen (who is in fact Snow White's stepmother) disguises herself as a friendly and innocent local village woman so that the princess will take a bite from the adulterated fruit. In this 19th-century German children's story Snow White lapses into a sort of deep sleep from which she cannot be awakened by her friends the Seven Dwarves. In the Labyrinth Jared gives Hoggle a peach to pass onto Sarah, and although he's reluctant to offer the sullied fruit to his new friend, when she says she's very hungry he does indeed give it to her. We know that the intention is that by eating this tainted treat Sarah will forget what she's looking for. When Sarah eagerly takes a chomp out of the peach there's an audible sound —it doesn't seem ripe as a fully grown, mature fruit would not make that noise. Quickly after this the outside world starts to spin for Sarah and she feels as if "everything's dancing" as her mind floats toward her waltzing music box trinket.

This part of Sarah's journey is patently based on the story of Adam and Eve that's in the Book of Genesis of the Bible. Although God has forbidden the pair from eating the fruit from the Tree of Knowledge, a serpent tricks Eve into plucking fruit from this tree, assuring her that by eating it her "eyes would be opened." Eve also gives the fruit to Adam and with this act they become aware of their own nakedness. This deed also results in Adam and Eve's expulsion from the Garden of Eden. In Sarah's case, by eating the fruit she drifts off to the Masquerade Ball.

## The Masquerade Ball

The guests at the Masquerade Ball are undoubtedly adults and very confident in their surroundings. This is at odds with Sarah who appears lost and although very beautifully dressed and made-up, she is a fish out of water there. Hence this adult world is both confusing and enticing in the same measure. Sarah sees Jareth and is mesmerized by him and the ballroom ambience— at least for a moment. This ball conceivably represents sexual awakenings since it follows the moment that Sarah takes a bite from the poisoned peach, an action which itself implies the loss of innocence. However, Sarah fights off her desires as she pushes through the other guests so that she may break free of this grown-up realm. This shows us that although Sarah has matured a great deal along the way, she does not need to enter the adult world too quickly and certainly will not relinquish Toby to Jareth for the sake of her own pleasure. Therefore, unlike Adam and Eve, Sarah is not banished from her own world but does leave with greater knowledge of herself. Finally, once Sarah lands back on ground we see that the peach contains a writhing maggot which displays its impure contents.

# 9 LOCATION, LOCATION, LOCATION

The Labyrinth is a myriad of weird and wonderful locations. Stone and hedge mazes form part of this world with the castle lying at the heart of the Labyrinth, located beyond Goblin City. These various environments offer challenges to Sarah on her expedition and are the homes of the Labyrinth's creatures, offering a context in which to understand these inhabitants. But the unusual and visionary settings Sarah stumbles upon are meaningful in their own right, giving us further clues to our heroine's chronicle.

## The Bog of Eternal Stench

The Bog of Eternal Stench is a festering and bubbling marsh-like place that is feared and avoided by most of the Labyrinth's inhabitants. The Bog burps, belches, and passes wind so we are given a palpable idea of what this swamp smells like. Hoggle is particularly terrified of this part of the Labyrinth and tells Sarah that even if her foot touches the Bog, she'll smell awful for the rest of her life—it doesn't *ever* wash off. The Bog is often used as a threat by Jareth to control Hoggle: "If she ever kisses you I'll turn you into a prince—Prince of the Land of Stench!"[10] and so this location acts as more than a mere region of the Labyrinth.

The word "swamp" means a boggy environment, but it can be used when speaking of emotions as well—to be 'swamped' in feelings is to be overwhelmed. The immense area that a swamp can encompass can denote feelings of hopelessness and helplessness. Hence, we may also understand the Bog of Eternal Stench as embodying Sarah's grief for her mother. If she becomes stuck in the Bog she may be trapped in hopelessness and not adequately process her grief. Furthermore, swamps symbolize the deepest, darkest aspects of ourselves that we keep hidden from others. Feelings of insecurity and embarrassment can be typified by this wetland. But swamps may also relate to potentials since these quagmires can be thought of as primordial and that from which life emerges. As with everything in the Labyrinth—creatures, locations, instructions—the Bog of Eternal Stench may not be just what it seems.

The Oubliette
An oubliette is a type of small dungeon with an opening at the top, rather than having a door as an entrance on ground level. Sarah falls into the oubliette after choosing to carry on the way down in the well of Helping Hands (previous chapter). Due to their small size and lack of light, oubliettes were more severe forms of punishment and torture than dungeons in medieval times. Traditionally they would be only large enough for one person to stand up in, so the prisoner couldn't sit, crouch, or even turn from side to side. You can imagine how torturous this would be, to have to stand for hours, days, weeks, and even months without respite. In the Labyrinth the oubliette is not quite this bad as Sarah does have room to sit and move around and there

---

[10] Labyrinth (1986). Directed by Jim Henson [Film]. USA: TriStar Pictures.

is even enough space for a visitor—Hoggle on this occasion. This chamber has been arranged by Jareth as a place for Sarah to forget about her mission to save Toby, not to cause her physical pain or persecution.

But Sarah does not want to forget—remembering a loved one that has passed on is an important aspect of dealing with grief. Merely trying to push aside memories and thoughts about someone who has left us (whether this be through death, abandonment, or a break-up in a relationship) is not a healthy way to grieve because this doesn't allow us to work through the emotions of such a loss. Remembering is important even if it causes emotional pain at first: by working through grief these recollections shouldn't be as upsetting in time. Therefore, Sarah's unwillingness to forget (Toby if taking the film at face value but perhaps also her mother in a more metaphorical sense) is a positive way to come to terms with such an enormous life transition.

## M. C. Escher Stairs

Stairs can signify both negative and positive aspects of life. Going up a set of stairs, can imply growth, development, and progress, with an increase in intelligence and awareness of the outer world, even a rise in confidence. But descending down a staircase can imply the internal conflict we have when life calls on us to mature and take on responsibilities, i.e. grow up. In the castle at the center of the Labyrinth, the stairs are very strange, going both up and down and the cases are perpendicular to one another. This is because these staircases are based on the artist M. C. Escher's lithograph entitled "Relativity." In this well-known illustration, figures are walking up and down the staircases and going about their daily business. To achieve this impossible depiction convincingly, Escher structured his drawing so that there were three distinct sources of gravity, each orthogonal to the remaining two. By doing this,

Escher tricks our perception of reality—every set of stairs works individually, but when the eye is drawn to another part of the lithograph, the mind is boggled at this optical illusion.

Sarah faces a great deal of conflicting emotions within the Labyrinth—the need to save her brother but the desire to hold her dreams in her hands; wanting life to be fair but appreciating that it often isn't; craving maturity but still needing the security of childhood. The way in which these seemingly contradictory needs can co-exist is reflected in this beautiful work by the Dutch artist. Perhaps Escher is telling us that we can be grown-ups but retain a youthful sense of innocence and imagination—life is rarely black or white.

# 10 A DREAM WITHIN A DREAM

In the course of Sarah's quest to retrieve her baby brother Toby from the clutches of the Goblin King Jareth, Sarah has made friends, solved puzzles, avoided certain death, and matured greatly. When we first saw Sarah, she was playing a game alone; now she has outwitted Jareth's most dastardly plots and even befriended one of the Labyrinth's most cynical residents (Hoggle).

Thus, despite the dangers untold and hardships unnumbered, Sarah did manage to fight her way to the castle beyond Goblin City. Although her newly found friends have helped her to come this far, she knows she must face this final confrontation alone, although it must be heartening that she knows she can call on Hoggle, Ludo, Didymous, and Ambrosius if needed. There comes a point in all our lives when we must stand on our own two feet and take on board adult obligations. Sarah is fully aware of this and now ready to meet Jareth and rescue Toby; in other words, Sarah is ready to move to the next more mature phase of her life. But she still must take a leap of faith to get to Toby, whom she can't seem to reach within the M. C. Escher stairs.

The Final Confrontation

Jareth is far from happy that Sarah has successfully navigated the Labyrinth, but yet he still covets her, or rather desperately wants her to adore him. Jareth points out all that he has done for Sarah (took the child, altered time, turned the world upside down, etc.) and beseeches her one final time: "I ask for so little—just let me rule you and you can have everything you want."[11] This is in essence a form of dictatorship and many such governments have existed throughout history. It's only when the people of a state realize that they in fact have dominion, not the dictator, that an uprising can occur and their world may change. It's possible for this shift in authority to happen at lower levels, in smaller communities, in families and even within a person him or herself.

If we remember at the beginning of the movie, before Sarah enters the Labyrinth, she couldn't remember the last sentence of her monologue when faced opposite the Goblin King. Although in the ultimate confrontation with Jareth she stumbles somewhat to find the line, the weight of realization that Sarah has control over her own life and can start making independent decisions about her path is clearly shown on her face when she quite rightly states: "You have no power over me."[11] This breaks Jareth's spell since people are only able to exert power over us (unless there is a particular vulnerability) if we allow them to.

Putting away childish things

When Sarah finally arrives back home, her transformation is complete as she takes Lancelot to Toby (who is back sleeping in his crib) and whispers to him that Lancelot is his now, while placing the toy in the baby's crib. Sarah puts

---

[11] Labyrinth (1986). Directed by Jim Henson [Film]. USA: TriStar Pictures.

away some of her childish things—toys, trinkets, and even her Labyrinth book—in her desk drawer. Sarah's growth reminds us of this passage:

*When I was a child, I used to speak like a child, think like a child, reason like a child; when I became a man, I did away with childish things. For now we see in a mirror dimly, but then face to face; now I know in part, but then I will know fully just as I also have been fully known. But now faith, hope, love, abide these three; but the greatest of these is love. 1 Cor. 13:11–13 New International Version New Testament*

Hence Sarah has matured so that she can put aside her childish emotions such as spite, anger, and jealousy—emotions that can harm others but achieve no real advantage for the individual. Sarah has overcome her resentment toward her brother, or, rather, regarding the loss of her mother, and is now able to love her family fully and have hope for the future.

But this doesn't mean she will not require help and support in the future. Sarah, looking rather forlorn, faces her mirror and sees her companions from the Labyrinth. Both Hoggle and Sir Didymus remind Sarah that if she should ever need them, they will be there. Sarah's final declaration is that she may indeed need all of her creatures, not for any particular reason but just because. Even as adults, it's ok to ask for help—we are only human and that's what friends are for.

One last thought on this parting scene—when Sarah was putting away her toys, she also took down and put away a picture of her mother. The owl, which we can consider as a representation of Sarah's mother, is now on the outside of the room and then flies away. Hence, Sarah has healthily processed her grief and can advance in her life, still remembering her mother but with love rather than anger at her abandonment.

## But what is the Labyrinth?

After all the discussion of topics and scenes in this book you may ask, "What is the Labyrinth"? The Labyrinth, quite simply, is life itself. So gather up some trusted friends, don't worry too much about decisions made, and enjoy the ride because—"All that we see or seem, is but a dream within a dream."[12]

---

[12] Poe, E.A. (1903). *The Works of Edgar Allan Poe, The Raven Edition, Volume 5.* New York: P. F. Collier and Son.

# ABOUT THE AUTHOR

Dr Megan Arroll (PhD, FHEA, CPsychol, CSci, AFBPsS) is a chartered psychologist and health researcher with a keen interest in invisible and misunderstood illnesses, integrative medicine and women's health. Megan currently holds the position of Senior Lecturer in Health Psychology at BPP University, Waterloo where she lectures on a range of topics including the psychology of health and illness, mental health and research methods. Meg is also rather obsessed with combining her knowledge of psychology and 1980s pop culture and has begun exploring the meaning behind classic 80s films and objects in her 'Psychology Of...' series. Follow on Twitter @DrMegHealthPsy

# DID YOU ENJOY THIS BOOK?

Maybe you have a different take on Sarah's journey through the Labyrinth—tweet thoughts to @DrMegHealthPsy

This is the first in my series of *The Psychology of...* books. Next:

## THE PSYCHOLOGY OF LEGO®

Do you now, or did you when you were a child, build the Lego® set obsessively, without deviating from the instructions? Or did you simply throw away the directions, instead preferring to make your own spaceship, house, or car? What does this say about you? The next book in *The Psychology of...* series unpicks the personality types and behaviors associated with the way people play with this famous toy and will also explore the trends Lego® has reflected the since the 1980s.

Can interlocking plastic brinks really tell us anything about ourselves...?

www.meganarroll.com

17060416R00030

Printed in Poland
by Amazon Fulfillment
Poland Sp. z o.o., Wrocław